What Did Jesus Command Us to Do?

Doug Roberts

What Did Jesus Command Us to Do?
by Doug Roberts

Copyright © 2017 Doug Roberts

Published by:

> *Doug Roberts Publishing*
> *P. O. Box 321*
> *Frederick, Oklahoma 73542*

Unless otherwise indicated, scripture quotations are taken from the New American Standard Bible® (NASB), Copyright © 1960, 1962, 1963, 1968, 1971, 1972, 1973, 1975, 1977, 1995 by The Lockman Foundation. Used by permission. www.Lockman.org

ISBN: 978-0-9825992-3-5

Printed in the United States of America

I want to thank Ed Chinn, Tim and Laurie Thornton, Shellie Kushnerick and Fred White for all the work they did in helping me transfer the things in my heart to print.

I want to say thank you to the most amazing woman, my wife Rita, who without her my journey would not have been complete.

Table of Contents

Chapter 1: The Great Commandment in the Law

"If you abide in Me, and My words abide in you, ask whatever you wish, and it shall be done for you. By this is My Father glorified, that you bear much fruit, and so prove to be My disciples. Just as the Father has loved Me, I have also loved you; abide in My love. If you keep My commandments, you will abide in My love; just as I have kept My Father's commandments, and abide in His love."

—John 15:7-10

Jesus didn't say, "If you keep My Father's commandments, you will abide in My love." He said, "If you keep *My* commandments you will abide in *My* love, just like *I've* kept the Father's commandment and abided in *His* love." So Jesus makes a differentiation here—a differentiation between what the Father commanded Him and what Jesus commands us.

Let me ask you a question, and it's a trick question: What are the two greatest commandments that Jesus gave us in the New Testament? Most people would say *to love the Lord your God with all your heart and all your soul, and to love your neighbor as yourself.*

But Jesus didn't command that.

Let's take a look at Matthew 22:34-39—"And one of them, a lawyer, asked Him a question, testing Him, 'Teacher, which is the great commandment in the Law?' And He said to him, 'You shall love the Lord your God with all your heart, and with all your soul, and with all your mind. This is the great and foremost commandment. The second is like it, You shall love your neighbor as yourself.'"

Notice what the lawyer asked: "Which is the great commandment *in the Law.*" Jesus answered the question that the lawyer asked. He answered with the great commandment in the Law. How many people can keep the Law? When I ask people what Jesus' greatest commandment was, most quote the Law that they can't keep. Do you see the trap?

Jesus Fulfills the Law

Jesus came to fulfill the commandments that God gave. Jesus kept the Law, and He fulfilled the Law. As a result, when God looks at us, He doesn't see us through the Law—He sees us through Christ. If we don't believe that, we have to get our minds renewed. We have to believe that Jesus fulfilled the

Jesus fulfilled the Law. So when God looks at us, He doesn't see us through the Law, He sees us in Christ.

commandments of God. We must believe in Him. Unfortunately, when we continue to think in old ways, we revert to the Law because religion dictates—and we've been taught—the Law. But we're no longer children of the Law—we're children of the Spirit! When Jesus fulfilled the Law He gave us access to the Father. So now, we no longer live according to the Law, we live according to Christ. We live in Christ and He says to us, "Now, go obey the things I've commanded you" (Matthew 28:20, my paraphrase).

When Jesus has another conversation in Mark 12 about the greatest commandment, one of the scribes jumps into the discussion with what Jesus describes as an "intelligent reply," and then Jesus says to him, "You're not far from the kingdom of God."

Well, if intelligence gets you "not far" from the kingdom, then I don't want to be intelligent. I want to be *in* the kingdom of God! Religion and the Law may get us close to the kingdom, but they don't get us *in* the kingdom because we can never keep the rules.

You see, the devil is always judging you through the Law because he knows you can't keep it. That's why you're always battling condemnation. But the Bible says, "There's now no condemnation for those who are in Christ Jesus" (Romans 8:1). So if you're battling condemnation, the first thing that tells me is that you're not abiding in Christ because in Christ, there is no condemnation.

If you're battling condemnation, the first thing that tells me is that you're not abiding in Christ because in Christ, there is no condemnation.

The flesh is never going to be able to please God, so if you're trying to please God in your flesh, just quit it. Die to your flesh. Walk in the Spirit because the only way you're going to please God is in the Spirit: "Those who worship Him must worship Him in spirit and in truth" (John 4:24).

Chapter 2: Being in Christ

We keep our focus on the flesh but the flesh is never going to be perfect, which is why the Scripture says that we don't know one another after the flesh anymore, but that we know one another after the Spirit (2 Cor 5:16). So I don't know you after the flesh, I know you after the Spirit. The flesh is always going to disappoint. The devil always tries to keep our relationships in the flesh because the flesh will never measure up. That's why we have divorce, that's why we have separation, and that's why we have division—because I'm never going to please your flesh and you can't please mine, either. I can't even please my own flesh! How can I then please yours?

Religion tries to keep our relationships in the flesh—Do this, do that, don't do this, don't do that.

Religion tries to keep our relationships in the flesh—do this, do that, don't do this, don't do that.

But we're spirit beings walking together in the Spirit. Our fellowship is in the Spirit of the Lord, not in the flesh of man. We're not children of the Law, but children of the promise! John 1:17 says, "the law was given through Moses; grace and truth

5

were realized through Jesus Christ." Galatians 4:31 tells us that "we are not children of a bondwoman, but of the free woman."

Who are we? We're children of God, and Jesus paid the price that we couldn't pay! He fulfilled what God required. I couldn't keep what God required. You couldn't keep what God required. But Jesus could and did!

Jesus fulfilled all the requirements of the Father! Now when the Father looks at us, He sees us in Christ—He sees who we are in Christ. He doesn't see us in the Law; He sees us in Christ. Aren't you glad?

Our Freedom in Christ

"Where the Spirit of the Lord is, there is liberty." (2 Cor 3:17)

Paul was constantly reminding his friends of their freedom in Christ. He wrote to the Galatians, "You foolish Galatians…Having begun by the Spirit, are you now being perfected by the flesh?" (3:1-3). And again, "It was for freedom that Christ set us free. Do not be subject again to a yoke of slavery" (5:1). Paul understood that the yoke of slavery is the Law. As we've seen in the last chapters, you're not children of the Law, you're children of the Spirit in Christ. As children of the

Spirit, you're going to keep the spirit of the Law because Christ, the fulfiller of the Law, is in you. You're not going to murder or do other things the Law forbids because those actions violate who you are.

You're going to keep the spirit of the Law, because Christ...is in you. You're not going to murder or do other things the law forbids because those actions violate who you are.

However, you don't measure yourself by the Law; you measure yourself by Christ. You don't measure yourself by me; you measure yourself by Christ.

Our Example and future is Christ

Jesus is our example. He is our model. Paul told the Corinthians to imitate his faith as he imitated, or followed, Christ. So he's teaching us how to be sons—how to walk in the Spirit—and he learned these ways from imitating Jesus. In other words, Paul tells all of us how to be what God has called us to be. He essentially says, "Watch what I do and do it."

If you look at what Paul teaches, they are not traditions. Paul wrote, "I press on in order that I may lay hold of that for which also I was laid hold of by Christ Jesus...forgetting what lies behind and reaching forward to what lies ahead" (Philippians 3: 12-13). We cannot forget what lies behind and reach forward to what lies ahead while we keep hanging onto traditions of men! Everything that lies ahead is new in Christ. Each one of you was called with a purpose that no one else can accomplish. You have a job to do and it lies ahead of you, not behind you.

Chapter 3: The First Commandment

In John 14:21, Jesus said, "He who has My commandments and keeps them is the one who loves Me; and he who loves Me will be loved by My Father, and I will love him and will disclose Myself to him." Think about that—if we keep His commandments, we will be loved by the Father and Jesus will disclose Himself to us. I think that's a good deal.

Now we're in Christ, fully clothed with Christ, walking in what Christ has predestined us to be with all the authority that the Father's given us. And because of that, we can love.

I know you love Him and I know you want to please Him, but we need to know what His commandments are in order to keep them. By now, we should know that His commandments are not found in the Law because we can't keep it.

Jesus gives us a key in John 15:14-16—"You are My friends if you do what I command you." I want to be Jesus' friend. I want to be loved by the Father. I want Jesus to reveal Himself to me, so I want to know what His commandments are. I don't care what man's commandments are. I only care what Jesus' commandments are.

When we know who Jesus is, He will tell us who we are, and then we can do the things He's commanded us to do. But the problem is that we really don't know what He's commanded us to do. We know what our doctrine tells us. We know what our tradition tells us. But what has *Jesus* told us?

He commands, in John 14:1, "believe in God, believe also in Me."

He didn't say that we believe *about* Jesus Christ. The devil believes about Jesus Christ; the demons believe about Jesus Christ. No, here it says that we believe *in* Christ. We believe in. Now we're in Christ, fully clothed with Christ, walking in what Christ has predestined us to be with all the authority that the Father's given us. And because of that, we can love.

In John 6:28-29, the multitude asked Jesus, "'What shall we do, so that we may work the works of God?' And Jesus said, 'This is the work of God, that you believe in Him whom He has sent.'"

So how do you do the works of God? By being in Him. How do we do the works of God? By just abiding in Him.

10

When He says to do something, we do something. When He says not to do something, we don't do that thing. Why? Because Jesus only did what He saw the Father do, and He only spoke what He heard from the Father. We talk a lot of times when we haven't heard anything from the Father. We preach a lot of things we have never heard, and our preaching is dead. It doesn't change anything. But when you speak what God has spoken, that word brings life—it brings fruit.

Chapter 4: Love as He Loves

So the first commandment is that we believe in Christ. The second commandment is "that you love one another, even as I have loved you[...]By this all men will know that you are My disciples, if you love one another" (John 13:34-35).

Now, let me ask you a question: Do you want me to love you the way I love myself? Or do you want me to love you the way Christ loved me? Now, if I love you the way I love myself and I'm having a bad day, you're out of luck. But if I love you the way Christ loved me, then I'm loving you unconditionally. I'm loving you if you don't even respond to my love. I'm loving you without expectations. I'm loving you without requirements. I'm even loving you if you do bad things to me. I'm even loving you if you curse me. I'm even loving you if you mistreat me. Why? Because that's what Jesus commanded. We're to love one another *the way He loved us*: unconditionally. Are we doing that?

We're too often loving like sinners love. How do sinners love? Well, you do good to me, I'll do good to you. You buy me a beer, I'll buy you a beer. Sinners do that. But we're to love like Christ loved us. If you never can do anything for me, I'm still going to bless you. If you can never repay, I'm still going to love you because that's how Christ loved me.

12

Even when I was not loving—when I was cursing Him, when I didn't believe in Him—He loved me. What changed my life was when I encountered His love. It wasn't when I encountered His

When you teach people who they are in Christ and they encounter the love of God, they're not going to go back to sin because there's no better place than in the love of God.

judgment. It wasn't when I encountered His rebuke. It was when I encountered His love, and His love changed me. It's the goodness of God—it's God loving us—that brings us to repentance.

Let me remind you that God's really not concerned about our sin. Of course, that doesn't give us the freedom to go sin. But when you teach people who they are in Christ and they encounter the love of God, they're not going to go back to sin because there's no better place than in the love of God. Who does not like love? Who does not respond to love?

The world is longing for the love of the Father. The world is longing for acceptance, for identity, for encouragement, for hope.

They're looking for it. That's why they do drugs. That's why they have sex outside of covenant and divine design. They hope to fulfill something that only Jesus can fulfill. There's only one place they can find it: in Him.

When you encounter the love of God, things change. You understand? We're ambassadors of love. When you call people into the love of God, His love is going to change them.

Chapter 5: Be Baptized in the Holy Spirit

The third thing Jesus commanded His disciples was that they be baptized in the Holy Spirit. Think about it. Here are the disciples, who had walked with and knew Jesus well, and then one day, Jesus says, "I've got to go. But I'm going to send Somebody; I'm going to send a Helper. I'm going to send the promise of the Father, the Holy Spirit. Don't do anything and don't go any place until you receive the Holy Spirit because you need the Holy Spirit to be able to fulfill your destiny" (see John 14).

Jesus commanded them, "Don't even try it without the Holy Spirit." Are we bigger than Jesus? He didn't even start His ministry on the earth until He was baptized in the Holy Spirit.

He says, "Don't even try it without the Holy Spirit."

Are we bigger than Jesus? Are we greater than his disciples? Jesus himself didn't even start His ministry on the earth until He was baptized in the Holy Spirit. When He was baptized in the water, a dove came and He was baptized in the Spirit. After that He was led into the wilderness and tempted by the devil. When He came out, He began His ministry.

Now, if Jesus needed the Holy Spirit, I think it's pretty clear that we also need the Holy Spirit. Maybe that's why it's one of His commandments.

Remember in John 14:16-17, Jesus said He would "ask the Father, and He will give you another Helper, that He may be with you forever; that is the Spirit of truth." That Helper and Spirit of Truth is the Holy Spirit. Jesus promises that "I will not leave you as orphans" (John 14:18).

One thing the Holy Spirit does is to bring us into an understanding of who we are in Christ. We will never fulfill our purpose without knowing who we are in Christ and without walking in our sonship with the Father.

More scriptures about the Holy Spirit

John 16:7 "But I tell you the truth, it is to your advantage that I go away; for if I do not go away, the Helper will not come to you; but if I go, I will send Him to you."

John 16:13 "When He, the Spirit of truth, comes, He will guide you into all truth; for He will not speak on His own initiative, but whatever He hears, He will speak; and He will disclose to you what is to come."

Acts 1:8 "But you shall receive power, when the Holy Spirit is come upon you; and you shall be my witnesses both in Jerusalem, and in all Judaea and Samaria, and unto the uttermost part of the earth."

The work of the Spirit

Acts 1:8   He gives us power.

Acts 9:31   He strengthens and encourages us.

Ephesians 1:13-14   He is the seal and deposit that guarantees our inheritance.

John 16:5-15   He convicts the world of sin, he guides us into all truth, he discloses to us what

    is to come, he glorifies Jesus, and he give to us what Jesus has for us.

Romans 8:26   He helps our weakness and makes intercession for us.

Acts 13:2   He calls men to service.

Luke 12:12   He teaches us.

Jude 20   He builds us up as we pray in the Holy Spirit.

Chapter 6: Go Make Disciples

In Matthew 28:19-20 Jesus tells us, "Go, therefore, and build a church—go and start a ministry, teaching them what your traditions of men are."

Is that what it says? No! It says, "Go therefore and make disciples of all the nations, baptizing them in the name of the Father, the Son, and the Holy Spirit, teaching them to observe all that I commanded you."

Jesus told us to make disciples and teach them to obey what He commanded. What did He teach His disciples? Who they were! He said, "I'll make you fishers of men" (Matt 4:19). He didn't teach them religion; He brought them into identity.

The commandment to go make disciples extends to us today. We are to go and make disciples of Christ. Paul said in Colossians that we are to bring every man complete into Christ. So if I'm discipling you, I've got to hear from the Father who Jesus says you are, and then I can disciple you into who He says you are. It might look completely different than who I am.

I pastor men that are businessmen, cowboys, musicians, and even farmers. They're all different. I also pastor pastors. But I don't try to make all of them alike because that's not what God's called them to be. I disciple them into who God has called them to be in Christ.

If two people are exactly alike, one of them is not needed. I mean, look at a family. Even identical twins have a uniqueness from each other, and most people look very different from each other. Why? Because they're all unique. They're all masterpieces, each made by the Father. Each of us has a different grace, a different call, and a different anointing. Each of us is important. Why? Because that's how God made us.

So, we're to make disciples, baptizing them in the name of the Father, the Son, and the Holy Spirit. We're not to just teach them about the Father, we're not to just teach them about Jesus, we're not to just teach them about the Holy Spirit—we are to bring them into the purpose of the life they're living. They need to know that they are formed in the Father, in Christ, and in the Holy Spirit.

That is how we are built together as the household of God. Where does God live? In us. How many houses does God have? One. In that house are many dwelling places. It's like your home. I'm sure you have a kitchen, a bathroom, a bedroom, a living room and other rooms. You only have one house, but many different rooms. The Father has one house, but many dwelling places—He dwells within each of us.

Chapter 7: Preach the Kingdom of God

Let's review what Jesus has commanded us to do:

1. Believe in Him
2. Love one another the way that He loved us.
3. Be baptized in the Holy Spirit.
4. Make disciples.

Let's read Luke 9:1-2 for the fifth commandment: "And He called the twelve together, and gave them power and authority over all the demons, and to heal diseases. And He sent them out to proclaim the kingdom of God, and to perform healing."

The fifth commandment is that we preach the kingdom of God. What is the kingdom of God? Are we preaching it? Or are we preaching church traditions?

The Gospel of the Kingdom is this:

1. God is your Father.
2. You are part of His family.

3. He wants to rule in you—He wants to dwell in you—in order for you to do the works that God has called you to do in Christ. You've got a purpose.
4. Begin to walk. Be a doer. Do what you believe.

Be a Doer

Here are some very large questions: Are you doing what you believe? Or are you just believing? Do you believe God saves? If so, are people getting saved around you? Do you believe God heals? If so, are people getting healed around you? Do you believe God wants to baptize in the Holy Spirit? If so, are people receiving the Holy Spirit around you? These things should be normal. Why? Because it's what God wants us to be doing. You're the only one that can do it.

A man once told me, "I'm praying that God will do something in my family."

I said, "Well, start."

He said, "I'm waiting for God to send someone."

I said, "He's already sent someone."

"Who did He send?"

"You."

Another time, a mother told me, "My children are on drugs."

I said, "Pray for them."

She said, "They won't let me."

I said, "They can't stop you."

When she seemed confused, I said, "Go into their bedroom, lay your hand on their pillow, say, 'Father, I pray that every time my child lays his head on this pillow he would dream the dreams that you have for him. I pray that every time he lays on this bed he would lay in the love that you have for him. I pray that he would encounter your presence. I pray he would come into the fullness of who he is in you.'"

Drugs are not the issue; identity is the issue. When you find your identity in Christ, everything else will take care of itself. Quit telling them they shouldn't do drugs and just tell them who they are in Christ. Bless them. Blessings do a lot more than curses.

Release the Holy Spirit to do His job. Release the Spirit of God to do what He wants to do.

When you find your identity in Christ, everything else will take care of itself. Quit telling them they shouldn't do drugs and just tell them who they are in Christ.

A pastor told me about a lady whose husband was a drunk. He was very mean. He wouldn't come to the Sunday morning service; he would just fight with her about it. So she asked the pastor, "What should I do?"

He said, "Go to the bar with him."

And, of course, she said, "Well, I can't go to the bar." He didn't say to go get drunk with him. He said, "Go to the bar with him and be a support. Just love him."

So the next Saturday night when her husband got ready to go to the bar, she said, "I'm going with you."

And he said, "I'm going to the bar."

She said, "I know. You're my husband and I want to support what you're doing."

24

So she went to the bar, sat at the table, and drank water. And while he was drinking his liquor, he got convicted because his wife loved him enough to support him in stuff she didn't even believe in.

Sunday morning, she woke up and started getting ready to go to church. Her husband said, "Wait a minute. I'm going with you."

She said, "Why?"

"Because you're my wife and I want to support what you're doing." He got saved and delivered and filled with the Holy Spirit. He's a leader in the church today because his wife loved him like Christ loved.

Love them out of their sin. Love covers a multitude of sins. Don't turn your freedom into an occasion to sin, but use your freedom to love one another. She submitted to her husband as unto the Lord, went to the bar, smiled, and encouraged her husband. He got convicted. Her attitude of blessing released the Holy Spirit to do His job.

That is the kingdom. Those are some of the principles of the kingdom. Quit preaching to people and just live who you are.

Your living is going to be more powerful than your speaking. I can say, "Sister, I love you." Does that mean anything to you? Nothing. But if I start showing my love, ministering, meeting her needs, she knows I love her, not because of my words but because of my actions.

God's called us to be lovers. Jesus said, Believe in Me. Love one another the way I loved you. Be baptized in the Holy Spirit. Make disciples. Preach the Gospel of the Kingdom. Heal the sick. Cast out demons.

Isn't it amazing that what Jesus commanded us to do is what religion and the devil are fighting against? Too often, religion tries to turn us into intellectuals instead of sons and daughters. Jesus said in John 5:39-40, "You search the Scriptures because you think that in them you have eternal life; it is these that testify about Me; and you are unwilling to come to Me so that you may have life."

Intellectualism will never get you into the eternal purposes of God. It's only believing in Christ; it's only living in Christ that can do that.

We often answer intellectually, but our intellect won't help us to know who Christ is. Intellectualism will never get you into the eternal purposes of God. It's only believing in Christ; it's only living in Christ that can do that. As Paul told the Athenians, "It's in Him we live and move and have our being."

This is who we are. When we stop intellectualizing and start *doing*, revival will start. Why? Because "the Father's word will not return until it accomplished what it was sent forth to do" (Isaiah 55:11, my paraphrase). We are the expression of the Father's word. When we hear from the Father and we step out in faith, we will not return until God accomplishes what He sent us to do.

The first question we need to ask the Lord: Who is Jesus to me?
The second: Who does Jesus say that I am?
The third: What does the Father have for me to do?

Are you going to do the things he has for you to do? If so, just tell the Lord, "Father, here I am. I understand what you've called

27

me to do. I yield to your purpose. Send me to do the works Jesus said to do. Ha, ha, ha, on you, devil! You're not going to rob my destiny. Here I come! In Jesus' name, Amen."

I've led more people to the Lord through a word of knowledge or a word of prophecy than almost anything else. I'll go up and ask somebody, "How are you doing?"

They usually say, "I'm doing great."

"If you're doing great, why haven't you forgiven your husband? If you're doing great, why are you still battling shame and condemnation?"

"How do you know that?"

"Because God loves you. He came to set you free. You need to know Jesus, the one that delivers you."

That's evangelism—using the gifts of God to reconcile the world to Himself.

1 Corinthians 2:9 tells us that our eyes have not seen and our ears has not heard all that God has prepared for those who believe.

Don't limit God anymore. Quit judging yourself. God believes in you. You're here because God chose you. He's appointed you to go and do the works of the Lord.

So do it.

Group Discussion Guide

My hope and purpose for this book is to see it become seed in the rich soil of human hearts. These questions were put together by some brothers and sisters to help you work these truths into your life.

1. Using Matthew 22:34-39, explain the difference between the way most people interpret "the two greatest commandments" and what Jesus said about them.

2. When God looks at us, does He see a lawbreaker? If so, why? If not, what does He see?

3. Why does our enemy (and religion) keep us focused on the law?

4. Yet, we are going to keep the spirit of the Law. Why? (Hint: It's not because of the slavery of the Law.)

5. What do you think the Apostle Paul meant when he told the Corinthians to "imitate me as I imitate Christ?" Who do you imitate as they imitate Christ?

6. What does it mean to be "in Christ"? What does that actually look like? Recall stories of personal experiences of being "in Christ."

7. Jesus said He only spoke what He heard from the Father. Why do we sometimes speak when we *haven't* heard the Father?

8. Chapter 4 says, "What changed my life was when I encountered His love. It wasn't when I encountered His judgment." Can you describe a specific time you have

encountered God's love? What did that do for you?

9. Explain the difference between the way Christ loves and the way the world loves.

10. You read in Chapter 4 that "God is really not concerned about our sin." Do you believe that? Why? Why not?

11. Why is being baptized in the Holy Spirit so important? Have you been baptized in the Holy Spirit?

12. In Chapter 6, we discussed the Great Commission: "Go make disciples…teaching them to observe all that I have commanded you." What things did Jesus command His disciples to do?

13. What is the "kingdom of God?" How is that different from Heaven?

14. Explain and respond to the statement in Chapter 7, "A false gospel of religious tradition—with all of its denominations and rules—has been preached. It says you can get saved and then wait around in a church building until you die. But the Gospel of the kingdom has not been sufficiently preached."

15. Why is the emphasis on "doing" so important?

16. Most people think that drugs are one of the biggest issues of our day. Yet, "Drugs are not the issue. Identity is the issue." What do you think that means?

17. Why do you think "religion tries to turn us into intellectuals instead of sons and daughters?"

18. This book closes with 1 Corinthians 2:9. What does that mean? Then pray that we may all stop limiting God in our

lives. Pray that we may firmly believe that He has appointed us to do the works of the Lord.

www.ingramcontent.com/pod-product-compliance
Lightning Source LLC
Chambersburg PA
CBHW032115040426

42337CB00041B/1408